boy

patrick phillips

THE VQR POETRY SERIES

Boy

THE

V Q R

POETRY
SERIES

Boy

POEMS BY PATRICK PHILLIPS

The University of Georgia Press   Athens and London

Published by The University of Georgia Press

Athens, Georgia 30602

© 2008 by Patrick Phillips

Set in Minion Pro

by Graphic Composition, Inc., Bogart, Georgia

Printed and bound by Thomson-Shore

The paper in this book meets the guidelines for

permanence and durability of the Committee on

Production Guidelines for Book Longevity of the

Council on Library Resources.

Printed in the United States of America

12   11   10   09   08   P   5   4   3   2   1

Library of Congress Cataloging-in-Publication Data

Phillips, Patrick, 1970–

Boy : poems / by Patrick Phillips.

       p.   cm. — (VQR poetry series)

Includes bibliographical references.

ISBN-13: 978-0-8203-3119-5 (pbk. : alk. paper)

ISBN-10: 0-8203-3119-8 (pbk. : alk paper)

1. Family—Poetry. I. Title.

PS3616.H465B69 2008

811'.6—dc22

2007039157

British Library Cataloging-in-Publication Data available

for my mother and father

and for Ellen

Contents

IV

Acknowledgments

Grateful acknowledgment is made to the editors of the following publications, in which these poems first appeared:

Cave Wall: "Our Situation," "Falling," "Poem about Sparrows"
Cortland Review: "A History of Twilight"
Greensboro Review: "Panegyric for Sid," "Matinee"
Harvard Review: "In the Beginning"
New England Review: "What Happens," "Everything," "At the End of the All-Night Drive"
Post Road: "Those Georgia Sundays," "Litany"
Shenandoah: "Ars Poetica"
Virginia Quarterly Review: "Fever," "Nathaniel," "Kitchen," "6:12"

"What Happens" appeared on the Poetry Daily Web site (poems.com), September 17, 2006
"Those Georgia Sundays" appeared in the anthology *Conversation Pieces,* edited by Kurt Brown, Alfred A. Knopf, 2007
"Matinee" appeared in the syndicated newspaper column "American Life in Poetry," selected by Ted Kooser, August 9, 2007
"Our Situation" appeared on the Verse Daily Web site (versedaily.org), September 7, 2007

For their friendship, guidance, and support, I am deeply grateful to Michael Collier, Jennifer Grotz, Kathy Graber, Rachel and Jeff Hayden, James Hoch, James and Paula Phillips, Billy Reynolds, Martha Rhodes, Tom Sleigh, and C. Dale Young. Special thanks to those who helped shape these poems into a book: Ellen Brazier, Brian Dempster, Merrill Feitell, Ted Genoways, and Kristin Henderson. Thanks also to Yaddo, the MacDowell Colony, Drew University, New York University, SUNY Maritime College, the Bread Loaf Writers' Conference, and everyone at the Virginia Quarterly Review and the University of Georgia Press. To Ellen, Sidney, and Cameron: *love, love, love.*

Boy

He that hath wife and children
hath given hostages to fortune.

—Francis Bacon

I

Revelation

Tim Mullinax and I
were setting army men on fire,

lobbing safety matches
at a whole platoon

waist-deep in kerosene,
when the purple flames

leapt up his arm
and around his throat

and coiled in his hair,
where, looking up,

I saw things clearly
for the first time in my life:

the perfect sky
still perfect as he burned.

Untitled

You won't believe it now,
but for two whole days
you were only the baby,
the boy,
the X-Man, Dr. Who.

I could barely stand it,
but your mother
was in no hurry
to decide whose eyes
cracked open, like a kitten,
as you nursed.

She cooed and kissed
and cupped your throbbing skull,
and lingered,
until they brought the yellow form,
in that moment
when we could have called you anything.

When you were you,
beloved,
and had no other name.

Fever

It is the year the sky reminds us
some mistakes cannot be mended.

The year, dime-eyed and listless,
a fever came to kill him.

Imperceptibly the windows
creep towards the floor,

the black bay whitening,
widening with the squall.

It is the night the lights
on the far shore hurtle backwards:

the drugstore, the hospital,
the sleeping doctors all

dissolving in the roar.
I want to ask the dark

who died and made me king:
three times I've filled the tub

and three times dipped him,
burning, in the water.

Not because I know what I am doing,
or because it helps,

but because the fathers and the mothers
whose job it is to save us

are all frail, or far away,
or gone forever to their graves.

It is the hour of nothingness,
and of that lamplit silence

in which sleep alone has the power
to bring my mother back,

a blue boy in her arms
as she whispers *Lord*

have mercy.
Lord have mercy on us.

Our Situation

In the dark we watch

our son's chest

rise and fall,

a balsawood airplane

still clutched in his fist

as he sleeps.

How reckless it seems.

How naïve:

to love a thing

so fragile and so weak.

What Happens

1

What happens never happens on its own.
The future and the past collide.

I've known a radio to go on playing
the song that it was playing

just before my father's Pontiac began to slide—
the past so stubbornly persistent

even Jimi Hendrix would not stop wailing
just because my face was broken

and the rain was blowing
through what had been a windshield—

spotlit figures clutching their knees
and sobbing in the grass

as Jimi shrieked and shrieked out of the past,
until finally I found the knob

I'd cranked in my euphoria, just before
the gods let loose their wrath.

2

And sometimes what happens
must happen more than once,

as when my friend died and the news
reached me in a cabin on a hillside,

where I presided over row
after row of sleeping campers.

Where a stranger whispered
through a moth-flecked screen,

then stayed with me,
talking about what happened

until there was nothing left but sleep.
But by the time I woke up,

I'd forgotten.
And I was showered, shaved

and halfway down the mountain
when a twig snapped, and he died.

3

And sometimes what happens
doesn't even happen,

like when it was time
for my wife to push

and she pushed so hard
the screen flatlined.

So hard the heart stopped
and the whole room began

to flash and beep, like on tv.
Nurses streamed through doors

and in an instant we were childless.
We wandered through our days.

The doctors worked and worked
and nothing happened.

And it was then I knew for sure
that nothing cares for us.

And I was changed.
And I have never been the same

though I've learned
to pretend I do not know

what can happen and unhappen
in no more time than it would take

an angel or a devil to descend into my wife
and pass through her into my son,

who was miraculously born into this world,
where everywhere and always

hearts are stopping for no reason.
And for no reason, starting up again.

Kitchen

I can see the grout between the bricks
and hear the Hot Wheel clatter
as it fishtails, and then flips.

The stove like some experiment:
clouds of sweet steam belching
each time my mother lifts
the stockpot's sweaty lid.

My sister's busy with her Barbies.
My brother in the fortress of his room.

So I alone sprawl at her feet—
the same age and in
exactly the same mood

as my son, now, in this kitchen
where soon we will
have lived so long ago.

II

Piano

Touched by your goodness, I am like
that grand piano we found one night on Willoughby
that someone had smashed and somehow
heaved through an open window.

And you might think by this I mean I'm broken
or abandoned, or unloved. Truth is, I don't
know exactly what I am, any more
than the wreckage in the alley knows
it's a piano, filling with trash and yellow leaves.

Maybe I'm all that's left of what I was.
But touching me, I know, you are the good
breeze blowing across its rusted strings.

What would you call that feeling when the wood,
even with its cracked harp, starts to sing?

Nathaniel

Whatever it was
    that made the Reverend
        Barker stoop that way,

it meant no matter
    how much he screamed
        at my friend Nathaniel

for being late, for not
    raking the leaves,
        or for raking the Goddamned

leaves the wrong Goddamned way,
    he could only ever scowl
        at the tops of his wing-tip shoes

or at the cuffs of the black wool suit
    he always seemed to be wearing
        when he'd thunder into the yard,

or down the stairs, or through
    the little speaker of some payphone
        we huddled around, *God*

damnit Nathaniel, I told you,
    I told you, Nathaniel, Goddamnit!
        his fury repeating

so precisely it became a joke
    we hollered through the halls,
        changing my friend's name

to Goddamnit Nathaniel, as in
    Where the hell's Goddamnit Nathaniel?
        I told you, Goddamnit, to get me a Coke!

which was stupid but funny at fourteen,
    and still just as stupidly funny at nineteen,
        when we'd yell across a bonfire

Don't bogart that joint Goddamnit
Nathaniel, Haven't I told you
    to pass the bong when you're through?

which is still funny to me even now—
    even though I look back and see,
        as I could not have seen then,

that Reverend Barker only stooped that way
    because he was dying,
        because cancer was eating his liver,

and because with each day
    it became both more urgent
        and more unlikely

that he would ever manage to say
    whatever it was he meant
        when he'd sit at the kitchen table,

or grip the black phone,
    or stand in the darkened driveway
      after we'd all gone home,

staring at the ground and saying nothing
    to his sweet, beloved boy
      but *Goddamnit*

Nathaniel, listen to me.
    Listen Goddamnit.
      Goddamnit Nathaniel, now listen.

Matinee

After the biopsy,
after the bonescan,
after the consult and the crying,

for a few hours no one could find them,
not even my sister,
because it turns out

they'd gone to the movies.
Something tragic was playing,
something epic,

and so they went to the comedy
with their popcorn
and their cokes—

the old wife whispering everything twice,
the old husband
cupping a palm to his ear,

as the late sun lit up an orchard
behind the strip mall,
and they sat in the dark holding hands.

At the End of the All-Night Drive

a woman who looks
almost exactly
like my mother
runs toward me, crying

and pointing
at a tangle of wires
that could be
my father, if only

he were made of dust
and full of holes—
though I can tell
the seeping tubes

and beeping screens
and people working on him
are all real:
working on him,

like people given
all the pieces and told
to make them
back into my father.

Though this isn't,
you understand, a story.
I see this. I am there
in the corner, watching

when they reach inside him.
And though there is
no way to explain it,
or tell you what I mean,

it's my voice that keeps
whispering *all right.*
It's alright, rocking
my sleeping mother in my arms.

Panegyric for Sid

The belly.

The belly
of the boy.

The glowing white
and gray ultrasound
of the head
and the legs
and the belly
of the shimmering
sea-horse-sized
boy.

The wet feet
and the knuckle-ish knees
and the cord
spilling from the womb,
still attached
to the heaving
white and then blue,
purple then red,
and then breathing pink belly
of the suddenly
unattached boy.

Belly on which
my hand rests
like a giant sculpture

of a hand
in the first photographs
of the milk-mounded,
black-cord-crusted belly
of the bloody,
just-circumcised boy.

Boy in the crook of my arm,
in the nest of my neck,
touching my stubbled,
rough cheek
as I lift the white shirt
and kiss the great
sack-in-your-hand
of the belly's
barely perceptible skin.

Boy that I was, boy
that all men
of all shapes
and all beauty
and all ugliness
were once—
unwittingly lovely,
unknowingly, unabashedly
granting the world
the long, smooth,
unassailable proof
there is good
in the bad universe,
good in the weightless
white fuzz,
good in the quiver

and the scowl
and the grin,
good
in the sleeping, full,
rising and falling
white belly
of the perfect
blond blur
of the beautiful boy.

The Fixer

They think I can fix anything
if I want to make it right:

broken trucks and cracked race-tracks
and crickets cupped too tight.

They think that I can fix the ruined
world. And so I do:

a perfect cricket flickering
from any hand they choose.

III

Everything

This is for everything left out in the rain.
For all that rusts in the dew.

For the light of the long-extinct star and the hole
in everything, everywhere it shines through.

This is for the splint and the chock and the shim
always offering their wings, their faint prayer.

For the bucket of limbs at Shiloh. For the boy
clutching a wound in the air.

This is for whatever, foredoomed and forsaken,
makes and then fails to make do.

For my child's stick-figure-filled heaven.
For the heavens we believed in once too.

This is for everything, everywhere turning to nothing.
For the sun, and for me, and for you.

Poem about Sparrows

Some of the sparrows
    had driven the bluebird
        from a nest they preferred to their own.

The worst of the bullies
    had come down from the feeder
        and gathered around it, and shrieked.

I remember believing something
    would stop them, as they hammered
        and hammered their beaks through its brain.

But instead, I stood watching
    the wet bead of its eyeball
        blinking and blinking, until it was blank.

Instead, I stood scrawling
    on the back of a letter,
        Poem about sparrows: Dachau, Bergen-Belsen.

Those Georgia Sundays

In Georgia, too, my father got up early,
wearing piss-stained boxers in the August heat,
then with yellow hands that reeked of Vantage
Ultra Light 100s, made the AC shudder.

Jesus Fucking Christ, I'd thank him
as he moaned, hacking and spitting in the john.
And when the toaster clunked, slowly
I would rise and make the sofa-bed,

knowing we had no time left, yet saying
nothing to him, all the way to our weekend job
waxing floors at Southern Bell.

What did I know? I knew damned well.
And even over the hum I heard death hiss
through those austere and lonely offices.

Sons and Brothers

When I see them on the playground, clawing
to get or keep some treasure or another,
bickering and bawling all
that's fair and unfair to their mother,

I can't help marveling that we
were like them once: each brother
a star locked inescapably
within the orbit of the other.

And though I want to still believe
that their embrace, in war and peace,
will go on that way forever,
these days when arm-in-arm we drink

at someone's wedding or another,
the past is what we scratch
and claw, and cannot keep,
though I was once your brother.

Parable

It's time for bed
she says,
pick your stories,

as I stack the plates
and cork the wine,

then turn again to the book
in which a man grieves
and grieves for his wife.

The chatter
from the bunkbed
slows, then stalls,

until it's clear
I'm the only one listening
to her voice
as it drifts down the stairs—

as the man in the book
falls to his knees,
searching for strands of black hair.

Ars Poetica

And even as their breath
froze beneath the stars,

as some clung
to the tilting deck

and some prayed to their gods,
a violin still quavered

a melody from Brahms—
not as a consolation,

or a sympathy, or solace,
but because the violinist

didn't know what else
to cling to

but his part in the sonata,
so that the living

would remember
all their lives, across the water,

that moment
when the sobbing cellist

grew very still
and raised his bow

and sent into the darkness
not a message, not a hope

but an almost imperceptible,
almost human moan.

Litany

Heavenly absence, I lift
my voice up to you

lifting it up unto nothing

and from the center
of the subdivision's maze,

O nothingness

I ask that you answer me
over the ratcheting chatter of the

meaningless

sprinklers, over the electric
hum of our

forsaken

lawns: O heavenly
indifference, whose moths are

senselessly

flinging themselves against the flood,
whose satellites drift

hopelessly

across the sky: my whole life
has been a dream

meaning nothing

of you—of wondering what it is
you mean to do with me, as I

pointlessly

mumble this, and close my eyes,
and feel your

not holy, not unholy

waters mist the night
with the sweet, sweet

meaningless

scent of all
I do not know.

IV

In the Beginning

we were cameras.
We opened our eyes
and dark leaves
fluttered in the wind.

We were little boxes
into which the air deposited
a barking dog,
the taste of honeysuckle,
the scent of something
rotting in the shadows
of a huge magnolia.

There was the world
and we were in it,
but all it meant was *world*.

When the endless dream
of childhood ended,
we were like dousing rods
that bowed and trembled
over everything.

We wanted to dig our graves
in the hearts
of those we loved
and lie down
in their skins.

And now, in the end,
we are like trees:
whole human beings
sprang from us!

We sway above them,
whispering things
not heard on earth
but in the dark
over such cribs.

Their gray eyes open
and our dark leaves
tremble in the wind.

6:12

My heart swelled inexplicably
when I turned the key

and caught the scent
of something lovely, coming from the kitchen.

I dropped my loaded bag
and clowned a heart attack

when my son came running from his room
and gripped my thumbs, and balanced on my shoes.

And as I broke into our nightly dance—
his graceless, middle-aged old man,

I knew: that I will be content
if this is all the heaven we are granted.

Living

I am living in the past
but it is not my own.

The future came to pass:
this future, where we're grown.

And yet my children only half
believe the youngest son

in the ancient photographs
is a boy I lived in once.

I laugh my father's laugh.
It has no other home.

The future is a myth.
And then it is a stone.

Falling

The truth is
that I fall in love

so easily because
it's easy. It happens

a dozen times some days.
I've lived whole lives,

had children,
grown old, and died

in the arms of other women
in no more time

than it takes the 2-train
to get from City Hall

to Brooklyn,
which always brings me

back to you:
the only one

I fall in love with
at least once every day—

not because
there are no other

lovely women in the world,
but because each time,

dying in their arms,
I call your name.

A History of Twilight

They are more fathers than sons themselves now.
—Donald Justice

When the sky is full of day each night
and all the little windows glow,
I lie back on a *Star Wars* pillow
and give the performance of my life:

playing the role of my father, reading
a bedtime story to my sons,
my voice so strangely his, it comes
to me: that such am I to them,

though to myself I'm still, forever
the one who shines over the book—
the bright boy shining a little brighter
every time his father looks.

Star Quilt

Those flowers that bloom
in the cotton are piss,

blood-cough of invalids,
vomit of infants,

and the dried cum-spots
of my forebears

preserved in a motley
of threadbare old scraps:

my whole inheritance
from the great-grandmother

who made it so
long ago, I can't tell you

which patch is a vestige
of a collar that soaked

the coke dust
from her husband's blue skin,

or which is the last
of the church-dress

she wore when they courted
in the summer of 1903:

when the war was unstarted
and the mirrors unshrouded,

and all the houses-to-burn
still unburned—

when everyone, everywhere
alive at this moment

was nothing,
and I myself was no more

than the seed of the seed
of the seed of a miner

and his tender bride, moaning
beneath these same stars.

Heaven

It will be the past
and we'll live there together.

Not as it was *to live*
but as it is remembered.

It will be the past.
We'll all go back together.

Everyone we ever loved,
and lost, and must remember.

It will be the past.
And it will last forever.

Notes

"Piano" is after William Meredith's "The Illiterate."

"Everything" is after the Danish poet Søren Ulrik Thomsen's "Tilegnet alt der har stået for længe i regnen" ("For everything left out too long in the rain").

"Those Georgia Sundays" is after Robert Hayden's "Those Winter Sundays."

"Parable" is after Jack Gilbert's "Married."